Contents

Words in **bold like this**, or in *italic like this*,
can be found in the glossary.

Vital air

The air in earth's atmosphere is vital to living things. Today, however, *pollution* produced by people is harming the air we breathe and damaging the rest of the natural world.

Our planet is surrounded by a layer of gases, like a blanket. This layer is called earth's atmosphere. The gases are more concentrated near the surface of the earth and less concentrated higher up. The main gas in the atmosphere is nitrogen. One-fifth of earth's atmosphere is made up of oxygen, which animals need to breathe.

Animals, including people, need a continual supply of oxygen. You cannot survive for much more than a minute without it. ▼

▲ Most air pollution comes from *power plants*, vehicles – such as cars and aeroplanes – and factories like this one in Brazil.

Polluted air

The clean, fresh air in earth's atmosphere is now being polluted (dirtied) by people. As we burn fuel in our homes, factories and cars, we add poisonous gases to the air. Air pollution can harm plants, animals and humans. It is even changing earth's climate.

TRY THIS!

The lichen test

How clean is the air where you live? One way of finding out is by looking at **lichens** growing on trees and stones. Some kinds of lichen form thick hairy growths. These only grow in clean air. Flat lichens can survive in polluted air.

Hairy lichen

Flat lichen

Natural cycles

Earth's atmosphere helps to regulate the weather. The make-up of gases in the atmosphere has stayed roughly the same for millions of years.

Plants and animals help to maintain the balance of gases in the air. Plants add oxygen to the air as they make their own food in a process called **photosynthesis**. They **absorb** carbon dioxide (CO_2) gas, water and minerals, and make sugars using sunlight energy. In the process, they release oxygen as waste. Animals absorb oxygen and give out carbon dioxide as they breathe.

Plants take in carbon dioxide and give off oxygen. Animals (such as deer) breathe in oxygen and release carbon dioxide as waste. ▼

The Greenhouse Effect

Sunlight heats the air in different parts of the earth unevenly. This produces weather of all kinds, including wind, rain, hail and snow. Gases in the air trap some of the sun's heat as it reflects back off earth's surface. The trapped heat generates warm conditions in which life can flourish. This is called the Greenhouse Effect. Air pollution made by humans means that more and more heat is trapped in the atmosphere. As a result, the temperature of the earth's surface is increasing.

TRY THIS!

Air and sunlight

Investigate the warming power of sunlight using three jars and a thermometer. Fill the jars with cold water and take the water temperature. Place one jar outside in the sun, another in the shade, and the third behind a pane of glass in the sun. After half an hour, test the water temperatures again. What do you find, and why? See page 31 for the answer.

◄ **As the sun heats the sea, tiny drops of water rise into the air to form clouds.**

weblinks

For more information about air pollution go to www.waylinks.co.uk/series/improving/air

What is pollution?

Pollution is any substance that harms nature. Pollution can affect water and the soil as well as the air. There are many different kinds of pollution, from fumes from a factory chimney to oil spills, and buried rubbish that harms the soil.

Any material that causes pollution is called a **pollutant**. Air pollutants include chemicals in the form of gases, and tiny **particles** of dust, ash and soot. Pollution can either be natural or made by people. Volcanic **eruptions** and fires started by lightning are natural events that produce pollution. An erupting volcano can shoot a giant cloud of ash and smoke into the air.

▲ When a volcano in the Philippine Islands called Mount Pinatubo erupted in 1991, it covered the region with a thick layer of ash.

▲ Factories, like this processing plant in Canada, are a major source of pollution.

Checking for pollution

Clean, fresh air has no smell or colour. Many kinds of pollution, such as smoke billowing from a bonfire, can be seen or smelled. However, some of the most dangerous types of pollution (such as **nuclear radiation**, see page 24) are invisible and have no smell. Scientists use special instruments to check for these sorts of pollution.

 KNOW THE FACTS

NATURAL DISASTER
The 1991 eruption of Mount Pinatubo produced so much dust and ash that it affected the world's weather. The ash cloud reduced the amount of sunlight that reached the earth for two years, which lowered temperatures by 3.5°C.

Industry and energy

The levels of different gases in the air have stayed about the same for thousands of years. Now people are upsetting the balance by producing pollution. Factories and power stations are two of the main sources of air pollution.

Factories and power plants produce pollution as they burn **fossil fuels** – coal, oil and gas – for energy. The waste gases produced when we burn fossil fuels include carbon dioxide, sulfur dioxide and nitrogen oxides. Factories may also give off smoke, dust, soot and poisonous chemicals.

The machines we rely on in our homes all use energy. Power stations cause pollution as they burn fuels to provide us with energy. ▼

A growing problem

For centuries, people have produced small amounts of pollution. For example, smoky fires have heated homes and blacksmiths' **forges** for thousands of years. In the nineteenth century, pollution increased as people invented machinery for manufacturing. The machines ran on fuels that produced pollution. Fuel-powered trains, ships and cars soon followed. During the twentieth century our use of machines increased, and human populations also grew. All this caused more pollution.

▲ **From the late eighteenth century, machines began to be used in manufacturing and mining. Chimneys belching smoke and soot were built in many places.**

TRY THIS! Soot from fuel

Soot and grime from industry now blacken buildings in many cities. To see how burning fuel produces pollution, ask an adult to hold an ovenproof dish over a lighted candle for a minute. Move the dish around slightly. Soot will soon appear on the underside.

Traffic pollution

Cars, trucks, trains, planes and ships all pollute the air as they burn fuels such as petrol and diesel. The problem is worst in crowded cities and near busy roads.

As vehicles burn fuel, they give off poisonous gases including carbon monoxide and nitrous oxides. Carbon monoxide can harm your health, and even kill you, by preventing your body from absorbing enough oxygen. This can make you feel sleepy or give you a headache. Nitrous oxides also cause **smog** (see page 14).

weblinks
For more information about traffic pollution go to www.waylinks.co.uk/series/improving/air

Planes that carry us to faraway places for holidays use much more fuel than cars, and produce far more pollution. ▼

Exhaust fumes

Lead is sometimes added to petrol to make vehicle engines run smoothly. Lead from car exhausts can harm people's kidneys, brain and nervous system. In **developed countries**, such as those in North America and in Europe, cars now run on lead-free petrol, which causes less pollution. They are also fitted with devices called **catalytic converters** that clean up exhaust fumes. But every year there are more and more cars on the road, so car pollution is still a big problem.

▲ Traffic in Kuala Lumpur, Malaysia: people in developing countries have fewer cars, but exhaust fumes still contain dangerous lead.

 TRY THIS!

Family car use

How much fuel does your family use in a week? Find out by keeping a record of all car journeys made in a week and noting down mileage. Are the roads busy or empty where you live? Driving in busy traffic uses up a lot of fuel. Are all your journeys really necessary?

KNOW THE FACTS

GAS GUZZLERS
People in developed countries have far more cars than people in poorer nations. For example, the USA has just 5 per cent of the world's population, but uses 43 per cent of all car fuel. If *developing countries* had as many cars, air pollution would become much worse.

Smoggy cities

In crowded cities, fumes from cars and factories can produce a poisonous haze called smog. In warm weather, when the problem is worst, thick smog can hide buildings and the surrounding landscape from view.

Smog forms when waste gases from car exhausts react with sunlight to produce a gas called **ozone**. High in the air, ozone can be helpful (see page 22), but near the ground it builds up to produce a foul-smelling haze. Smog is a major problem in cities such as Los Angeles and Mexico City, which lie in bowl-shaped valleys that trap the dirty air.

▲ Smog in Mexico City: the problem is worst in summer, when sunlight reacts with exhaust fumes during the long, daylight hours. The reaction releases dangerous gases that can damage people's lungs.

Health problems

Air poisoned with smog may harm your health. It can make your eyes and throat sore, and cause **allergic** reactions. Some people, including many children, suffer from **asthma** and other breathing problems. In certain cities the problem is so bad that people sometimes have to stay indoors or wear a mask.

◄ **Smog hangs over the city of Los Angeles in the USA.**

TAKE CARE!

Masks for cyclists

In many cities, smog and traffic fumes cause problems for cyclists. If you cycle in a busy city centre, you may need to wear a mask over your nose and mouth. This filters the air and stops you breathing in harmful fumes.

Acid rain

Life-giving rain is vital for animals and plants, including crops that provide us with food. But the rain in many regions is being made acidic by air pollution. Acid rain harms living things and even eats into stone.

Acid rain occurs when waste gases from power plants, cars and factories mix with water vapour in the air to make a weak acid. The tiny drops of polluted water form clouds, which later shed their moisture as acid rain, sleet or snow. Acid rain harms plants and drains off into rivers and lakes, where it kills water creatures such as fish.

◄ Trees damaged by acid rain shed their leaves and are more likely to die from disease.

KNOW THE FACTS

POISONED LAKES
In Sweden, experts report that 20,000 lakes have been poisoned by acid rain caused by pollution from factories in the UK, Germany and Poland.

Drifting on the wind

Strong winds can carry clouds containing acid rain a long way from the source of pollution. Thousands of trees in Canada have been poisoned by pollution from the USA. Lakes and **wetlands** damaged by acid rain can be sprayed with lime, which **neutralizes** the acid. However, this treatment is expensive and only lasts for a few years.

▲ A helicopter sprays lime on a lake in Sweden to counteract the effects of acid rain.

TRY THIS! **Acid damage**

Acid rain can damage stone, such as limestone, used in buildings. To see how acid eats away at the stone, put a stick of chalk into a jar containing vinegar. Vinegar works more quickly than acid rain because it is more acidic, and chalk is softer than stone, but the effect of the acid on the chalk is similar to that of acid rain on buildings and monuments.

weblinks
For more information about acid rain go to www.waylinks.co.uk/series/ improving/air

Global warming

Earth's climate is slowly but steadily getting warmer. This is the result of a problem known as *global warming*. Scientists have discovered that air pollution is to blame.

weblinks
For more information about global warming go to www.waylinks.co.uk/series/improving/air

As cars, factories and power plants burn fuel, they release waste gases which are trapping more of the sun's heat. This is increasing the natural Greenhouse Effect (see pages 6-7) and making the planet overheat. The main gas responsible for this is carbon dioxide (CO_2), which is released when fossil fuels and wood are burned. Nitrous oxides and methane are also greenhouse gases. Methane is given off by swamps, rice fields, and by animals digesting their food.

The ice at the *polar regions* and in glaciers is starting to melt because of global warming. This is adding more water to the oceans. The photo shows ice melting at the North Pole. ▼

Rising waters

During the twentieth century, the earth's temperature rose by 0.5°C. Temperatures may increase by another 2-3°C by the year 2100. The warm weather is making the polar ice-caps melt and the oceans expand. This is making sea levels rise. Global warming brings the risk of floods to low-lying areas. If it continues, coastal regions such as the Netherlands and Bangladesh could end up underwater.

▲ Rising sea levels add to the risk of floods in low-lying countries such as the Netherlands.

HELPING OUT
Saving energy

Power stations that burn fuel to supply us with energy release huge amounts of greenhouse gases. We can all help to slow down global warming by using less energy. There are a number of different ways we can do this. For example, make sure you turn off the lights when you are not in a room. Remember to switch off your TV and computer when you have finished using them. Leaving machines on stand-by uses almost as much energy as leaving them on altogether.

 KNOW THE FACTS

The wealthy nations of the world use much more energy and produce more greenhouse gases than poorer nations. The chart below shows the world's five biggest producers of carbon dioxide.

Tonnes of carbon dioxide released per person per year in 2000-1

USA	19.0
Australia	16.9
Canada	13.7
UK	9.5
Japan	9.3

Changing weather

Global warming is starting to make the weather wilder and more extreme in many places. Floods are occurring more often and there is a greater risk of *drought*.

Scientists believe that global warming is changing the world's weather. Dry regions such as parts of Africa and Australia seem to be getting even drier, which makes disasters such as droughts and fires more likely. Elsewhere, wet places are becoming wetter and suffering more floods. These changes make it harder for farmers in some areas to grow crops.

▲ Hurricanes, or violent storms, form over warm seas and cause damage like this when they sweep inland. Global warming could make hurricanes more common.

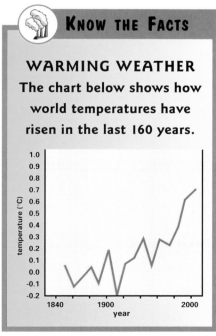

◀ Small anemone-like creatures called coral polyps build coral reefs. The polyps only thrive in water that is warm, but not too hot.

Animal homes

In future, global warming may threaten the survival of animals that live in particular **habitats**, such as scrub-lands, marshes or the polar regions. If conditions become unsuitable where the animals live, there may be nowhere else for them to go. Warming temperatures in the oceans threaten sea creatures, such as coral polyps, that build coral reefs. These reefs provide important habitats for many sea creatures.

KNOW THE FACTS

WARMING WEATHER
The chart below shows how world temperatures have risen in the last 160 years.

Ozone loss

High in the earth's atmosphere, a layer of ozone gas shields us from harmful rays in sunlight. In the last twenty years, scientists have discovered that air pollution is damaging this protective layer.

Ozone is a colourless gas, a form of oxygen. The ozone layer in the atmosphere is located about 25 kilometres (15 miles) above the earth's surface and screens us from the sun's harmful **ultraviolet (UV) rays**. These UV rays damage plants and animals and can cause skin cancer and eye damage in humans. In the 1980s, scientists discovered that ozone 'holes' or areas of reduced ozone were appearing over the polar regions each year. Ozone is also getting thinner in other parts of the world, too.

▲ **The ozone 'hole' over Antarctica shows up in dark blue in this image, taken by satellite in 2003.**

Repairing the damage

Experts soon realized that chemicals called **chlorofluorocarbons (CFCs)** were causing the damage. These chemicals were used in the manufacture of refrigerators, spray cans and some fast-food packaging. In 1987, countries around the world agreed to stop using the dangerous chemicals. Scientists expect the ozone layer to recover gradually over the next fifty years.

weblinks
For more information about the ozone layer go to www.waylinks.co.uk/series/improving/air

TAKE CARE!

Cover up!

Damage to the ozone layer means that it is more important than ever to protect yourself against the sun's harmful rays. Wear a hat and put on suntan lotion or a T-shirt in warm, sunny weather, especially when you are on the beach where there is little shade.

◀ **Old refrigerators containing CFCs have to be dismantled (taken apart) carefully, so the dangerous chemicals are not released into the atmosphere.**

The global threat

Some kinds of air pollution, such as smoking a cigarette, happen deliberately. But air pollution produced by one cigarette is small. Some of the worst cases of air pollution have happened because of accidents. Whether deliberate or accidental, the global threat from air pollution is huge.

In 1986, an accident at the nuclear plant near Chernobyl in Ukraine (below) caused an explosion that spread harmful radiation over much of Europe. ▼

Nuclear power plants use the energy created by splitting atoms of a rare metal called uranium to generate electricity. Uranium gives off dangerous **radiation** and is used to make nuclear weapons. In the last sixty years, deadly **radioactive** pollution has spread as a result of the exploding and testing of nuclear weapons. Accidents at nuclear power plants in Russia, the USA and Japan have also released clouds of dangerous radiation.

Burning forests

In parts of the developing world, farmers need more land to grow crops to feed their families. They clear forests using a method called 'slash-and-burn'. When the trees have been felled, the farmers chop the leaves and branches and let them dry out. They then use them to start fires to clear the area. The widespread practice of 'slash-and-burn' harms the atmosphere by filling the air with huge clouds of smoke.

▲ **People have cut down and burned this forest land in Liberia, West Africa, to make new fields for farming.**

 KNOW THE FACTS

FOREST INTO FARMLAND
Thirty per cent of the world's forests have now been turned into farmland, which is affecting the balance of gases in the atmosphere. Fewer trees means that less oxygen is produced and less carbon dioxide (CO_2) is absorbed. When trees are burned, more CO_2 is released.

TAKE CARE!

The dangers of smoking

Smoking cigarettes can cause serious illnesses such as heart disease and lung cancer. Smoking can harm not only the person smoking, but also people nearby who breathe in the smoke. Avoid breathing in other people's cigarette smoke. It is best never to start smoking, because once you do, it's very hard to stop.

25

Tackling air pollution

One way to tackle air pollution is to clean up the damage done. But the best way is to produce less pollution in the first place. All over the world, governments, scientists and ordinary people are now working to tackle pollution.

Global warming is the most serious environmental problem facing the world today. Since the 1990s, countries have met at conferences called Earth Summits to try to find ways of solving the crisis. At the Kyoto Summit in Japan in 1997, representatives drew up a plan to reduce the release of greenhouse gases by 5 per cent by 2012. However the USA and Russia have refused to sign the agreement because they believe it may harm their industries.

Wind farms, like this one in Wales in the UK, provide energy without polluting the atmosphere. Unlike fossil fuels, these energy sources won't run out. ▼

◄ This *solar-powered* car in California, USA, is having its battery recharged. Electric cars like this one do not use petrol and do not pollute the atmosphere.

'Clean' energy

Global warming is mainly caused by burning fossil fuels, so we can help to slow it down by using other forms of energy. Sunlight, wind and flowing water contain energy that can be used to generate electricity without causing pollution. These fuels are the way forward. Governments can raise money to fund research into clean energy by taxing motorists and fining companies that cause pollution.

HELPING OUT

Saving petrol

Every family can help to cut air pollution by using petrol more carefully. Ask your parents to save fuel by driving a little more slowly, or by having a smaller car.

Taking part

Everyone can help to reduce air pollution by using energy more carefully, so that fewer fossil fuels are burned. Travelling by bus or train instead of by car also cuts air pollution and saves precious fuel.

Saving energy at home and at school is easy – just switch off lights and machines such as TVs, stereos and computers when you're not using them. Turning down the central heating or air conditioning just a little can save a lot of energy. Simple things like not leaving the refrigerator door open, taking a shower instead of a bath, or using less water when you boil a kettle can all help.

▲ **If we all travel everywhere by car, we use a lot of fuel and this damages the environment. Taking the bus to school saves fuel and means less pollution.**

Recycling

The packaging that protects food and other goods we buy in shops uses energy and materials to make. When the food is unwrapped, most of the packaging just goes straight in the bin. Recycling glass, tins, cardboard, plastic and other packaging saves energy and natural resources. When you can, buy recycled products such as paper and toilet rolls. It may not seem like a lot, but if we all start making small changes we can help to make a big difference.

◄ **Recycling plastic, glass and tins is a good way of helping to save energy. Ask your school to start a recycling scheme if it doesn't have one already, and try to buy products that use less packaging.**

HELPING OUT

Share a ride

Help to reduce your family's car use by walking or riding a bike to school, or taking the school bus. If none of these methods is possible, ask your parents if you can share the ride with a friend.

Glossary

absorb take in.

allergic when the body reacts to a substance as if it is dangerous.

asthma an illness affecting the lungs and airways, which makes breathing difficult.

catalytic converter a device fitted to a car's exhaust system to reduce the pollution given off.

chlorofluorocarbons (CFCs) chemicals used in the manufacture of refrigerators, aerosol sprays and foam packaging, which harm the ozone layer.

developed countries the richer countries of the world, whose industries are well-developed. Developed countries include the USA, Canada, many European countries, Australia and Japan.

developing countries the poorer nations of the world, whose industries are less well developed. Developing nations include many countries in Africa, Asia and South America.

drought a long period of time without rain.

eruption when lava, ash and gas are released by a volcano.

forge a workshop where metal is heated to make horseshoes or tools.

fossil fuels fuels, such as coal and gas, made from the fossilized remains of plants and animals, found underground.

global warming the warming of weather worldwide, mainly caused by burning fossil fuels.

habitat a particular type of environment in which a plant or an animal lives.

lichen a living thing that is a combination of a fungus and an alga.

neutralize to counteract or make harmless.

nuclear having to do with atoms and their nuclei (central part) or with atomic energy.

nuclear radiation the rays produced as a result of the break-up of atoms.

ozone a form of oxygen. A layer of ozone gas in the atmosphere protects us from harmful (UV) rays in sunlight.

particles tiny units of matter, such as atoms.

photosynthesis the process by which plants make food using carbon dioxide from the air, sunlight energy and water.

polar regions the regions surrounding the North and South poles.

pollutant a substance that harms the air, water or land when released.

pollution any harmful substance that damages the environment.

power plant a factory where energy is generated/made.

radiation rays and particles produced when atoms are split.

radioactive giving off radiation and energy through the break-up of atoms.

smog a poisonous haze caused by vehicles' exhaust fumes.

solar-powered powered by energy made from sunlight.

ultraviolet (UV) rays radiation given off by the sun, which tans and also burns our skin.

wetland an area of fresh water, such as a stream, river, lake, marsh or pond.

Further information

Reading

Air Pollution by Matthew Chapman and Rob Bowden
(Wayland, 2001)
Changing Climate by Jen Green (Chrysalis/Belitha, 2003)
Climate Crisis by Nigel Hawkes (Franklin Watts, 2000)
Global Pollution by Paul Brown (Heinemann, 2002)
Polluted Planet by Jen Green (Chrysalis/Belitha, 2004)

Campaign Groups

Friends of the Earth
26-28 Underwood Street,
London N1 7JQ
Website: http://www.foe.co.uk

Air Pollution Websites

http://www.cleanairprogress.org/classroom/index.asp
Get friends and family to take the clean air challenge.

http://www.lungsandiego.org/environment/kids.asp
Information about how air pollution can affect people's health.

http://www.oneworld.net/penguin/pollution/pollution_home.html
Find out about all types of pollution.

http://www.defra.gov.uk/environment/climatechange/schools/
7-11/index.htm
UK government site on global warming

http://www.climnet.org/publicawareness/index.htm
Find out what you can do to stop climate change.

---

page 7
Answer: The water in the jar left in the sun will be warmer than the water
in the jar left in the shade, because the sun will have warmed the water
in the sunlit jar. The jar behind the pane of glass will be warmest of all,
because glass makes the sun's rays stronger.

Index

Numbers in **bold** refer to illustrations.